Dear Family,

What's the best way to help your child love reading?

Find good books like this one to share—and read together!

Here are some tips.

•**Take a "picture walk."** Look at all the pictures before you read. Talk about what you see.

•**Take turns.** Read to your child. Ham it up! Use different voices for different characters, and read with feeling! Then listen as your child reads to you, or explains the story in his or her own words.

•**Point out words as you read.** Help your child notice how letters and sounds go together. Point out unusual or difficult words that your child might not know. Talk about those words and what they mean.

•**Ask questions.** Stop to ask questions as you read. For example: "What do you think will happen next?" "How would you feel if that happened to you?"

•**Read every day.** Good stories are worth reading more than once! Read signs, labels, and even cereal boxes with your child. Visit the library to take out more books. And look for other JUST FOR YOU! BOOKS you and your child can share!

The Editors

For Regina—good lookin' out.
And for ezralang—the low-down dirtiest.
—DBB

For Tony Jacobson,
a good person and a great friend.
—AB

Text copyright © 2004 by Derrick D. Barnes.
Illustrations copyright © 2004 by Aaron Boyd.
Produced for Scholastic by COLOR-BRIDGE BOOKS, LLC, Brooklyn, NY
All rights reserved. Published by SCHOLASTIC INC.
JUST FOR YOU! is a trademark of Scholastic Inc.

Library of Congress Cataloging-in-Publication Data

Barnes, Derrick D.
    The low-down, bad-day blues / by Derrick D. Barnes ; illustrated by Aaron Boyd.
        p. cm.—(Just for you! Level 1)
    Summary: On a day when everything seems to be going wrong, from cloudy skies
to the cancellation of a favorite cartoon, a boy discovers what a difference his
attitude can make. Includes activity ideas for parents and children.
    ISBN 0-439-56867-6 (pbk.)
    [1. Attitude (Psychology)—Fiction. 2. African Americans—Fiction. 3. Stories
in rhyme.] I. Boyd, Aaron, 1971- ill. II. Title. III. Series.
    PZ8.3.B25217Lo 2004
    [E]—dc22

                                                                                    2004042915

16 15   16 17 18 19/0
        Printed in the U.S.A. 40 • First Scholastic Printing, February 2004

The Low-Down, Bad-Day Blues

by Derrick D. Barnes

Illustrated by Aaron Boyd

▲▲▲▲ JUST FOR YOU!™ ▲▲▲▲
▲▲ Level 1 ▲▲

The sun is hiding.
The sky is all gray.

No kickball, no baseball,
and no park today.

I got mud on my shoes.
My bike has a flat!

I got caught in the rain,
and I ruined my hat.

Low-Down Dirty, Bad-Day Blues!
I got the Low-Down,
Bad-Day Blues!

My tooth is loose.

There's a hole in my sock.

I'm the bluest kid
who lives on my block.

I lost my pet frog,
old Big Bubba-Ben.

My favorite cartoon
just went crazy again!

Low-Down Dirty, Bad-Day Blues!
I got the Low-Down, Bad-Day Blues!

I'm in big trouble now.
I got sent to my room!

I put dishwashing soap
in my sister's perfume!

I broke a joystick
to my video game.

I taped it,

and glued it,

but it's still not the same.

Low-Down Dirty,
Bad-Day Blues!
  I got the Low-Down,
  Bad-Day Blues!

My dog up and left me.
Things sure are tough!

I'm too young for these problems.
ENOUGH IS ENOUGH!

What's this?

The sky's getting clear.
The rain went away.

It's about time for some sunshine!
I've been blue the whole day.

My mom made a cake,
and she brought me a slice.

She said, "Go out and play,
and be sure to play nice!"

Daddy fixed my flat tire.

My dog came back!

I went to my closet
for a brand new hat.

I met all my buddies
at the park to play.

I waited it out,
and those blues went away.

That's right!

I had the Low-Down Dirty,
Bad-Day Blues.

But if you wait it out,
you just can't lose!

Here are some fun things for you to do.

Bye-Bye, Blues!

When people have the **blues**, they feel really bad!

Why does the boy get the blues?

Read all the bad things that happened to him.

Would YOU have the blues if those things happened to you?

When does the boy stop feeling blue?

Read all the good things that happened to him.

Now draw a picture of YOU feeling blue.

Show what makes you feel bad.

Then draw a picture of you feeling happy.
Show what makes YOU feel good!

One Lost Frog!

The boy's dog came back.
What about his frog,
old Big Bubba-Ben?
Do YOU think the boy
will ever find him?

Make up a new story!
Tell where the frog went.
Draw pictures to go with
your story.

▲▲▲▲TOGETHER TIME ▲▲▲▲

Make some time to share ideas about the story with your young reader! Here are some activities you can try. There are no right or wrong answers!

Talk About It: Talk more about what it means to "have the blues." Ask your child, "How do you feel about rainy days? Do they give you the blues or do you like them? How do sunny days make you feel? Why?"

Read It Again: Many famous musicians have played "The Blues!" When singers sing the blues, they may linger on the vowels in the words, or add a beat or a *"humph"* sound at the end of a phrase. Read the story again. This time you and your child can try singing the words as if you are singing a blues song! Stretch out the vowel sounds in words like *shoes, blues, loose, room,* and *perfume.* Invite your child to clap out the beat as you sing the words together.

Read More: Visit your local library to find other books about the blues and music, such as *How Sweet the Sound, African-American Songs for Children*, compiled by Wade and Cheryl Hudson, or *Harlem* and *The Blues of Flats Brown* by Walter Dean Myers. You may even want to check out some blues music to listen to.

Meet the Author

DERRICK D. BARNES says, "I live in the land of the low-down dirtiest blues and jazz in the country—New Orleans, Louisiana. Also, I can play a mean harmonica! (Well, sort of.) The music I listen to inspires my writing, and it's great to live in a place where I have so much good music all around me."

Derrick is a native of Kansas City, Missouri, but he spent a good portion of his growing up years in Mississippi. He is a graduate of Jackson State University, where he earned his degree in Marketing. He has worked as a copywriter for Hallmark Cards, and he had a brief career writing an advice column. He currently lives (and writes) in New Orleans with his wife, Tinka, and their son Ezra. *The Low-Down, Bad-Day Blues* is his first children's book. *Stop, Drop, and Chill!* is another book he has written in the JUST FOR YOU! series.

Meet the Artist

AARON BOYD says, "When I was six years old, I knew that I wanted to illustrate children's books. That's when I read *Strega Nona* by Tomie dePaola. I took that book out of my school library every week. I copied the pictures until I could draw the whole book from memory!"

Aaron has been an illustrator for more than ten years. He likes to draw stories about animals, and he especially likes to work on books with multicultural themes. Aaron thinks it is important for stories to reflect all the different kinds of people around us. He lives in Milwaukee, Wisconsin, with his best friend, his dog Queen. His other book in the JUST FOR YOU! series is *I Can't Take a Bath!*